A Guide for Using

Alexander and the Terrible, Horrible, No Good, Very Bad Day

in the Classroom

*Based on the book written by **Judith Viorst***

*This guide was written by **Diane Porteous, M.A. Ed.*** *and illustrated by **Bruce Hedges***

Teacher Created Materials, Inc.
6421 Industry Way
Westminster, CA 92683
www.teachercreated.com

©1998 Teacher Created Materials
Reprinted, 2001
Made in U.S.A.
ISBN 1-57690-347-8

Table of Contents

Introduction

A good book can touch the lives of children like a good friend. Great care has been taken in selecting the books and activities featured in the Literature Unit series. All the activities in this unit are intended for use with primary students, grades one to three. Some activities may need to be modified to meet the needs of students at various levels of ability. (Several modification options are included in the Suggestions for Using the Unit Activities.) Activities in all academic subjects have been incorporated to make this a unit which teaches and reinforces skills across the curriculum. It is hoped that students will enjoy the story and feel a kinship with Alexander, while gaining knowledge and skills in all areas.

Teachers who use the activities to supplement their own ideas can choose one of the following methods.

A Sample Lesson Plan

The sample lesson plan on page four provides you with a specific set of lesson suggestions. Each of the lessons suggested can take from one to several days to complete and can include all or some of the suggested activities. Refer to the Suggestions for Using the Unit Activities on pages 7–13 for information relating to unit activities.

A Unit Planner

If you wish to tailor the suggestions on pages 7–13 to a format other than that prescribed on the next page, use the Unit Planner on page five. On a specific day, you may choose the activities you wish to include by writing the activity number or a brief notation about the lesson in the Unit Activities section. Space has also been provided for other related notes and comments. Reproduce copies of page five as needed.

Sample Lesson Plan

Lesson 1

- Introduce the book by using any or all of the Before the Book activities.
- Read the story orally to the students.
- Ask some of the story questions (page 20) after reading the book.
- Have the students write in their journals about the worst day they ever had.

Lesson 2

- Have the students read the story orally to you in small groups and/or with a partner.
- Continue to ask some of the story questions on page 20.
- Read "The Alexander Rap" together (page 26). See suggestions pertaining to rap music on page 8.
- With the whole class, use the sequencing strips to put story events in order. (pages 18 and 19)
- Have students individually complete the Get the Scoop! sequencing activity. (page 27)

Lesson 3

- Read *Today Was a Terrible Day* by Patricia Reilly Giff orally to the class.
- Compare and contrast Alexander and Ronald Morgan and the things that happen to them in the stories.
- Have students complete the story map (page 25) for either or both of the stories.
- Share the information from Getting to Know the Book and Author with students. (page 6)
- Have students complete the gym shoe homophone worksheet. (page 28)

Lesson 4

- Orally read to the class *Alexander Who's Not (Do you hear me? I mean it!) Going to Move.*
- If available, read *Ira Says Goodbye* and/or *Mitchell Is Moving* also.

- Compare and contrast the stories.
- Have students write in their journals about the good and bad things about moving.
- Have students do A Neighborhood Grid Map activity. (page 35)
- Have students draw a floor plan for Alexander's new bedroom.
- Use the map on page 40 to help children discover how far away 1,000 miles is.

Lesson 5

- Orally read to the class *Alexander, Who Used to Be Rich Last Sunday.*
- Using enlarged coins, do the money math problems while reading the story.
- Have students do the Time for Lunch! activity. (page 29)
- Have a garage sale.

Lesson 6

- Have students complete the map of Australia (page 39) by reading the clues given.
- Help students learn about Australian animals by doing the Aussie Animals cut-and-paste activity. (page 41)
- Show the National Geographic video *Wonders Down Under.*

Lesson 7

- Have children participate in Readers' Theater by performing the play "Alexander Goes Down Under." (page 43)
- Sing the song "Alexander Was Having a Bad Day." (page 46)
- Have students do the A Sundae on Sunday activity (page 32). This involves actually making and eating sundaes.
- Watch the HBO video *Alexander and the Terrible, Horrible, No Good, Very Bad Day.* (See bibliography, page 48.)

Unit Planner

Unit Activities

Date:

Notes/Comments:

Unit Activities

Date:

Notes/Comments:

Unit Activities

Date:

Notes/Comments:

Unit Activities

Date:

Notes/Comments:

Unit Activities

Date:

Notes/Comments:

Unit Activities

Date:

Notes/Comments:

Getting to Know the Book and the Author

About the Book

Alexander and the Terrible, Horrible, No Good, Very Bad Day, written by Judith Viorst, has been well-known and well-loved by children and adults alike for over two decades. Alexander is a typical boy of about seven or eight years old who has "one of those days" when nothing goes right. At the same time, everything seems to be going very well for everyone else, including his brothers who get prizes in their breakfast cereal and cool new pairs of shoes while his friends at school get praised by their teacher and have dessert in their lunches. Alexander, of course, gets none of these things. Several times he claims he is going to move to Australia, which gets no response from anyone until the end of the book when his mother tells him that there are bad days "even in Australia." Children can easily relate to Alexander's experiences and feelings and will enjoy reading this book over and over.

About the Author

Judith Stahl Viorst was born in Newark, New Jersey, on February 2, 1931. She grew up in New Jersey and graduated from Rutgers University. She married Milton Viorst, a political reporter and writer, in January 1960. They live in the Washington, D.C., area and have three grown sons—Anthony, Nicholas, and Alexander.

Judith Viorst has wanted to be a writer since she was a child. She has written many poems, books, and articles for children and adults. She started writing poems, most of them gloomy ones about death and suicide, which were promptly rejected by publishers. She began editing science books for teenagers and then wrote a few paperback science books, which launched her career as a published author.

Most of Viorst's poetry and fiction books come from her own life experiences. Her sons are characters in several of her books, including *Alexander and the Terrible, Horrible, No Good, Very Bad Day, Alexander, Who Used to be Rich Last Sunday,* and *Alexander Who's Not (Do you hear me? I mean it!) Going to Move,* all featured in this literature unit. She wrote *I'll Fix Anthony* and *My Mama Says There Aren't Any Zombies, Ghosts, Vampires, Creatures, Demons, Monsters, Fiends, Goblins, or Things* for her son Nick who was having problems with his older brother and with fears of monsters. *The Tenth Good Thing About Barney,* for which she received the Golden Pencil Award in 1973, was written in response to questions her children were raising about death. Ms. Viorst continues to enjoy writing for people of all ages.

Suggestions for Using the Unit Activities

Use some or all of these suggestions to help children understand and appreciate the story, as well as to introduce, reinforce, and extend skills across the curriculum. The suggested activities have been divided into three sections to assist the teacher in planning the literature unit.

The sections are as follows:

- *Before the Book*—which includes suggestions for preparing the classroom environment and the students for the literature to be read.

- *Into the Book*—which has activities that focus on the book's content, characters, theme, etc.

- *After the Book*—which extends the reader's enjoyment of the book.

Before the Book

1. Use *Alexander and the Terrible, Horrible, No Good, Very Bad Day* and *Today Was a Terrible Day* by Patricia Reilly Giff (see Bibliography—Related Literature, page 48) in conjunction with the study of friends, families, and feelings. Both books lend themselves to discussions about what children can do when they have feelings of frustration and anger and how family members and friends can help them deal with those feelings. Sharing these books with children also offers the opportunity for students to think about how they can be helpful and understanding when someone they care about is having a difficult time. *Alexander and the Terrible, Horrible, No Good, Very Bad Day* also presents a wonderful opportunity to introduce children to the continent of Australia. The book *Alexander, Who Used to Be Rich Last Sunday* gives children a chance to practice counting coins and think about spending money wisely. *Alexander, Who's Not (Do you hear me? I mean it!) Going to Move* can help children understand and express feelings about moving to a new neighborhood. This book also lends itself to the study of neighborhoods and beginning United States geography.

2. Introduce the vocabulary to the students by doing any of the following:

- Print the words on ice-cream cone patterns (see page 17) and read them aloud together.

- Print the words on chart paper.

- Write the words in sentences on sentence strips. Read the sentences orally together to help children understand their meanings in context.

- Duplicate the list on page 14 and distribute it to students. Have them identify and write the compound words from the list onto the shoes at the bottom of the page.

Suggestions for Using the Unit
Activities *(cont.)*

Before the Book *(cont.)*

3. Before reading the story to the class, ask students if they have ever had a day when everything went wrong. Allow them to share some of their bad day experiences.

4. Show students the cover of the book and read them the title. Ask if any of them have heard or read the story before. Ask those who are unfamiliar with the story to predict what they think might happen to Alexander in the story.

Into the Book

Language Arts

1. Read the story aloud to the students. Stop at strategic points and ask them to predict what will happen next, such as when Alexander opens his lunch at school, when he goes to the shoe store, and when he goes to the dentist. Allow students to chime in chorally with you when reading, "It was a terrible, horrible, no good, very bad day."

2. Use the story questions on page 20 to check understanding of the story and to generate discussion.

3. Duplicate and cut apart the story summary sequencing strips on pages 18 and 19. Mount them on tagboard or sentence strips and laminate them. Place the strips in a pocket chart randomly and have volunteers arrange them sequentially according to the story. Or you can pass strips out to individual students, have them stand in a line in random order facing the rest of the class, and then individually read the sentence on the strip. Ask other students who have remained seated to arrange the children holding the strips in sequential order. You may wish to leave the sentence strips at the Alexander Center (see page 47) later for individual use.

4. As a review of the above activity, pass out copies of Get the Scoop! page 27. Have the children make an eight-decker ice-cream cone showing the sequential order of events in the story.

   (**Note:** Two events listed on the sentence strips are left out of this activity.) You may or may not wish to leave the sentence strips displayed in a pocket chart or on the blackboard chalk tray. Many children will want to number the scoops before they begin cutting and pasting. It may also be easier for some children to sequence the events from bottom to top. You may wish to allow this. The directions specify top-to-bottom order because it makes more sense to read them this way when finished. These ice-cream cones can be displayed when finished by punching a hole in the top scoop and tying a piece of string or yarn through the hole for hanging.

5. Read "The Alexander Rap" (page 26) together. This is more fun for students if you use background rap music. Appropriate instrumental-only rap music is available on cassette tape and will provide a steady beat. (See the bibliography, page 48.) **Note:** You can turn many poems into "raps" by playing rhythmical music when reading them. This is often very motivating for students.

        8   *© Teacher Created Materials, Inc.*

Suggestions for Using the Unit Activities *(cont.)*

Into the Book *(cont.)*

Language Arts

If you have no instrumental rap music tapes available, an easy way to add music and rhythm to poetry reading is to use a small electronic keyboard. (Your school music teacher may have one you can borrow.) The keyboard can automatically play a constant beat in various styles such as calypso or rock, and students will often become more interested in reading poetry. Reading "The Alexander Rap" may be easier for some children to do than reading the story independently. You may wish to make this an alternate reading assignment. You can also make reading the rap easier for students by dividing the class into two groups. Have more able students read the first four lines of verses one through seven and less able readers do the last two lines of each of those verses. Have all students read the last verse together.

6. Read *Today Was a Terrible Day* by Patricia Really Giff orally to students, or have them read it to you. Have students compare and contrast the main character, Ronald Morgan, with Alexander, as well as comparing the events in the two stories.

7. Have students complete the story map on page 25 to summarize *Alexander and the Terrible, Horrible, No Good, Very Bad Day*. This story map can also be used with *Today Was a Terrible Day* (see above) and Viorst's other Alexander books—*Alexander, Who Used to Be Rich Last Sunday* and *Alexander, Who's Not (Do you hear me? I mean it!) Going to Move*. In addition, it can become a prewriting activity for students to use when writing their own stories about Alexander. Several suggestions for journal and creative writing ideas appear on page 24.

8. Share all or part of the Getting to Know the Book and the Author section on page 6 with students. They will be interested to know that Alexander, Nicholas, and Anthony really are Judith Viorst's sons who are now grown. Have students find the date of publication of this book (1972) and help them figure out how long ago it was written as well as the approximate ages of the Viorst brothers now.

9. Children can practice and become familiar with various homophone pairs by completing the gym-shoe worksheet on page 28. **Note:** At least one word from each pair is found somewhere in the story. You may want to have the students find them. This can become a game by dividing the class into teams and setting a time limit. Have teams find as many of the homophones listed on the sheet as they can, noting the sentences where they are located in the story.

10. Share the story *Alexander, Who's Not (Do you hear me? I mean it!) Going to Move* with the class. Show them the cover and read the title. Have volunteers who are not familiar with the story predict what will happen. You may want to have children vote whether they think Alexander will or won't move and record the vote. After reading the story, see how many children were correct. Two other related books worth sharing with children at this time are *Ira Says Goodbye* by Bernard Waber and *Mitchell Is Moving* by Marjorie Weinman Sharmat. (See the bibliography, page 48). All three books are about moving and offer an excellent opportunity for comparing and contrasting.

Suggestions for Using the Unit Activities *(cont.)*

Into the Book *(cont.)*

Language Arts

11. You may want to have students write and/or draw about the good and bad things about moving. See the Social Studies section (page 11) for more suggested activities related to these books.

Math

1. Orally read to your class *Alexander, Who Used to Be Rich Last Sunday*. In this story, Alexander and his two brothers each receive $1.00 in various coin combinations from their grandparents. Alexander squanders his on silly items until he has no money left. While reading the story, do the money math with the class. An excellent way to do this with the whole class is to use enlarged coins in a pocket chart. If your chalkboard is magnetic, the coins can be "magnetized" on the back. Long rolls of peel-off sticky magnetic strips are available at many craft stores. Large cardboard or tagboard coins are often available in bulletin board sets at teacher supply stores or in catalogs. If you have difficulty finding readymade enlarged coins, you could make your own by photocopying real coins, enlarging them, mounting them on tagboard, and then laminating them.

2. Use the Time for Lunch! activity and/or the A Sundae on Sunday activity (pages 29–33) to give children practice counting coins to $1.00. Both activities are designed so that it is difficult, if not impossible, to come up with a combination of exactly $1.00. In the Time for Lunch! activity, children "buy" an imaginary lunch by cutting and pasting foods of their choice. In A Sundae on Sunday, children "buy" and make their own sundaes using real ingredients. (Getting to eat the results is often quite motivating!) In both activities each child receives one strip of coins (page 31) containing four each of quarters, dimes, nickels, and pennies. Children then cut and paste the exact coins needed to "pay" for their lunch or sundae. Children will often want to approach this differently. Some will want to cut and paste coins for the amount of each item and then count the coins for their total. Others will want to add the prices for all items and then cut and paste the coins for the total. Children using the first method sometimes run out of a particular kind of coin, especially pennies, and ask for more. Instruct them that they have more than enough coins to pay for their lunch or sundae but may have to do some "trading" to get the right answer. Either method is acceptable. The ability to problem-solve and get the correct result is the key. You may find it helpful to have a parent or an aide assist you during these activities. **Note:** A recipe for making "Tin Can Ice Cream" is included on page 34 so that your students can make their own ice cream and then use it to make their sundaes. If your students do make tin can ice cream, you can tie in a little science while making it by discussing how matter can change states from a liquid to a solid and vice versa.

Suggestions for Using the Unit Activities *(cont.)*

Into the Book *(cont.)*

Math

3. After reading about Alexander's disappointment at the shoe store, you can do a simple graphing activity with your students. You'll need a large piece of vinyl or plastic—a shower curtain liner will work. Mark it off into a grid with a permanent marker, making squares approximately 9–12 inches. Have students sit in a circle and take off one shoe and gently place it in the center of the circle. Choose a student or students to sort the shoes. This can be done several times as there are several ways they can be sorted, such as by color, style, brand name, laces/no laces, right/left, etc. Once sorted, the shoes can be "graphed" by placing them in rows on the vinyl graph. If you wish, this real-object graph can be made into a corresponding bar graph, using appropriately sized graph paper with squares ½" to 1".

4. Students can also make a favorite ice-cream graph. Duplicate the ice-cream cone pattern on page 17. (You may wish to reduce it somewhat.) Give one to each child. Have them color the ice-cream scoop to indicate their favorite ice-cream flavor. The cones can then be glued to a large piece of bulletin board paper or butcher paper in rows of like flavors. You may wish to limit the possibilities to four or five, such as chocolate, vanilla, strawberry, chocolate chip, and "other." This "pictograph" can be transferred to graph paper, making a corresponding bar graph. You can make up problems to go with the graph, such as "How many more children all together like vanilla and strawberry?" or "How many more children like chocolate than strawberry?"

5. In the story *Alexander, Who Used to Be Rich Last Sunday*, Alexander buys some useless items at a garage sale. Your students can have their own garage sale in your classroom. Have each student bring in one or two unwanted items—an old toy, game, or book that is not broken or damaged and still can be used. Duplicate several copies of the coins on page 31. Children can "earn" money over a period of time (a week or so) by following classroom rules, completing homework, being kind to others, etc. Allow students to "buy" items with their money at the garage sale. You may wish to allow students to take turns being the "sellers."

Social Studies

1. Pages 36 and 37, About Australia, are provided to give the teacher some background information about the country. You may wish to read all or part of this section to your students; however, learning about Australia will be more meaningful if children are allowed to explore and discover on their own, using the activities in the unit and reading some of the many excellent books available on Australia. (See the bibliography, page 48.)

2. Start by helping the children locate Australia on a world map. Distribute a copy of page 39 to the students. Have them read the clues and label Australia's states and territories. This can be done individually, with partners, in small groups, or as a whole class activity.

Suggestions for Using the Unit Activities *(cont.)*

Into the Book *(cont.)*

Social Studies

3. Have children complete A Neighborhood Grid Map on page 35 to practice locating coordinates. Various businesses and locations are taken from *Alexander and the Terrible, Horrible, No Good, Very Bad Day* and *Alexander, Who's Not (Do you hear me? I mean it!) Going to Move.* Using your large vinyl grid, you can have children practice finding coordinates before doing this activity. With masking tape or peel-off labels, mark the squares going down the sides with letters and those going across the bottom with numbers. Put some kind of treat (a piece of candy, a box of raisins, etc.) in each square. Make a card for each of the coordinates (A1, C3, B6, etc.) and distribute them to the children randomly. Let students go one at a time to the grid to find and take the treat at the coordinate on their card. This activity works best if there are more coordinates (and treats) than students so that the last few students still have several possibilities and must make some effort to find their own coordinates.

4. In *Alexander, Who's Not (Do you hear me? I mean it!) Going to Move*, the family is making preparations to move 1,000 miles away. Help your students understand how far 1,000 miles is by using the map on page 40 or any other United States map with a mileage scale. You may want to have some students use a large wall map while others use a smaller one. Give each child, or pair of children, a piece of yarn or string. Have them use the scale to measure a length representing 1,000 miles according to their scale. Children can pretend Alexander lives in their neighborhood. Have them place one end of the string as close to your town or city as possible and then rotate the string around to find different locations that are 1,000 miles from you. Help them to understand that the scales are relative to the map size and that they should find many of the same locations, regardless of the size of the map they are using. Have them record some of their locations on the back of their map and/or share them with the class to be recorded on the board or chart paper.

5. After sharing *Alexander, Who's Not . . . Moving* and/or either of the other related books (see #10, Language Arts section, page 9), you can have children draw floor plans. It is suggested in the Alexander Center Activities (page 47) that students draw a floor plan for Alexander's new bedroom. They can also draw a floor plan of their own bedrooms, one of Mitchell's new house (from *Mitchell Is Moving*), or Reggie's new house from *Ira Says Goodbye*. Help students understand that floor plans are drawn using a "bird's-eye view," as if they are stuck on the ceiling, looking down.

Suggestions for Using the Unit
Activities *(cont.)*

Into the Book *(cont.)*

Science

1. Students can discover much about Australia's unique animal life by completing the Aussie Animals cut-and-paste activity on pages 41 and 42. They simply match the picture with its description.

2. If at all possible after completing the Aussie Animals activity, rent, borrow, or purchase the National Geographic video *Wonders Down Under* from their Really Wild Animals series. (See the bibliography, page 48.) It is as entertaining as it is informative and features all the animals contained in the cut-and-paste activity.

After the Book

1. You may wish to use the Tin Can Ice Cream and/or A Sundae on Sunday activities as a culmination to the unit. (See math suggestion #2, page 10.)

2. Show the HBO video *Alexander and the Terrible, Horrible, No Good, Very Bad Day*. (See the bibliography, page 48.) You may want to do this while eating your sundaes.

3. Readers' Theater is a good way to help students connect drama and literature. They can either act out any of the Alexander stories or the play "Alexander Goes Down Under," included in this unit (pages 43–45), which presents and reinforces information learned about Australia. You may want to have the students perform the play for parents and/or other students. Stick puppets can be used instead of student actors. Prepare a stick puppet stage according to the directions on page 21. The puppet patterns on pages 22 and 23 can be used to dramatize Viorst's Alexander stories. Some additional puppets would be needed for "Alexander Goes Down Under."

4. With your students, sing the song "Alexander Was Having a Bad Day," (page 46). It is sung to the tune of "My Bonnie Lies Over the Ocean," a song with which most teachers and children are familiar. You may be able to have your music teacher tape-record piano accompaniment (no words) on a cassette tape. It is available, along with accompaniment for many other commonly known children's songs, from Book Lures. (See the bibliography, page 48.)

5. The Alexander Center Activities can be set up at a desk or a table. Provide drawing paper, writing paper, pencils, crayons, markers, paste, etc. You may also wish to display some play money and some of the books from the unit.

Vocabulary List

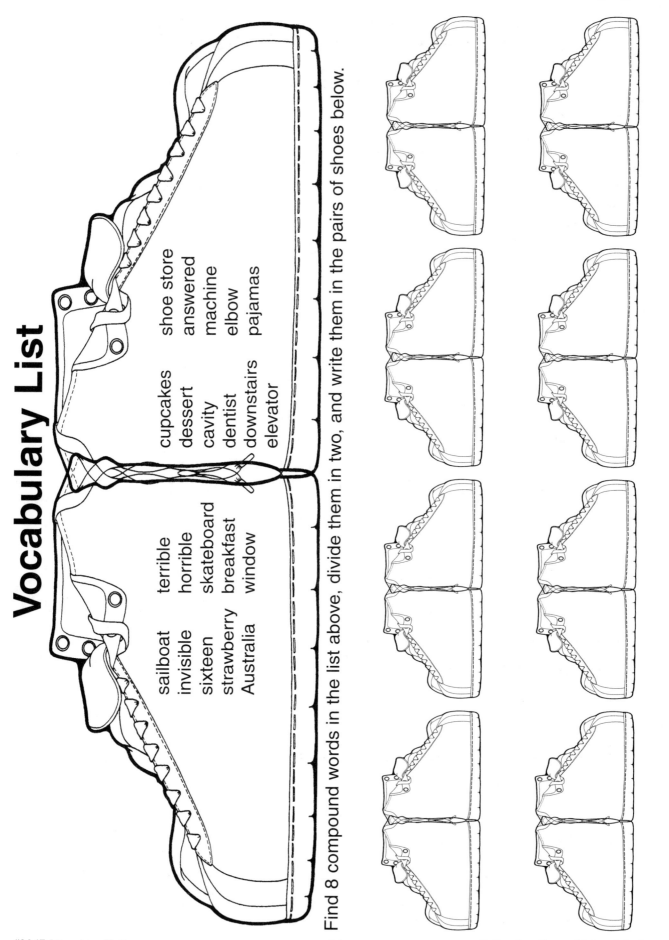

sailboat	terrible
invisible	horrible
sixteen	skateboard
strawberry	breakfast
Australia	window

cupcakes	shoe store
dessert	answered
cavity	machine
dentist	elbow
downstairs	pajamas
elevator	

Find 8 compound words in the list above, divide them in two, and write them in the pairs of shoes below.

Pocket Chart Activities

Prepare a pocket chart for storing and using the vocabulary cards, the story question cards, and the sentence strips.

How to Make a Pocket Chart

If a commercial pocket chart is unavailable, you can make a pocket chart if you have access to a laminator. Begin by laminating a 24" x 36" (60 cm x 90 cm) piece of colored tagboard. Run about 20" (50 cm) of additional plastic. To make nine pockets, cut the clear plastic into nine equal strips. Space the strips equally down the 36" (90 cm) length of the tagboard. Attach each strip with cellophane tape along the bottom and sides. This will hold sentence strips, word cards, etc., and can be displayed in a learning center or mounted on a chalk tray for use with a group. When your pocket chart is ready, use it to display the sentence strips, vocabulary words, and question cards. A sample chart is provided below.

How to Use the Pocket Chart

1. On cardstock or heavy paper, reproduce the ice-cream cone pattern on page 17. Write a vocabulary word from page 14 on each one and/or any other words from the story which you want your students to learn. It may be helpful to write sentences containing these words on sentence strips to help children use context clues to identify and understand the new vocabulary.

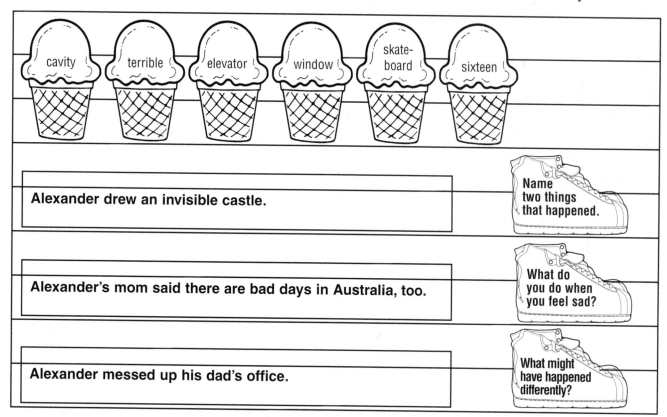

The pocket chart patterns can be used to make "Amazing Author," "Wonderful Worker," "Great Reader," and other appropriate awards or incentives.

Pocket Chart Activities *(cont.)*

How to Use the Pocket Chart *(cont.)*

2. Reproduce several copies of the shoe pattern on page17 on six different colors of paper. Use a different paper color to represent each of Bloom's Levels of Learning.

For example:

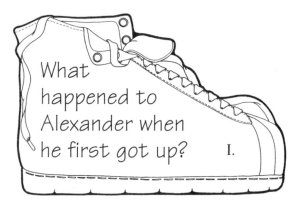

   I. Knowledge (*green*)

  II. Comprehension (*pink*)

 III. Application (*lavender*)

 IV. Analysis (*orange*)

  V. Synthesis (*blue*)

 VI. Evaluation (*yellow*)

Write a story question from page 20 on the appropriate color-coded shoe pattern. Write the level of the question and the question on the shoe, as shown in the example above.

Use the cards (shoes) after the corresponding pages have been read to provide opportunities for the children to develop and practice higher-level critical thinking skills. The cards can be used with some or all of the following activities:

> • Use a specific color-coded set of cards to question students at a particular level of learning.

> • Have a child choose a card and read it aloud or give it to the teacher to read aloud. The child answers the questions or calls on a volunteer to answer it.

> • Pair the children. The teacher reads a question. Partners take turns responding to the question.

> • Play a game. Divide the class into teams. Ask for a response to a question written on one of the question cards. Teams score a point for each appropriate response. If question cards have been prepared for several different stories, mix up the cards and ask team members to respond by naming the story that relates to the question. Extra points can be awarded if a team member answers the question also.

3. Use the sentence strips to practice oral reading and sequencing of the story events. Reproduce pages 18 and 19. If possible, laminate the sentence strips for durability. Cut out the sentence strips or prepare sentences of your own to use with the pocket chart.

Pocket Chart Patterns

Shoe

Ice Cream Cone

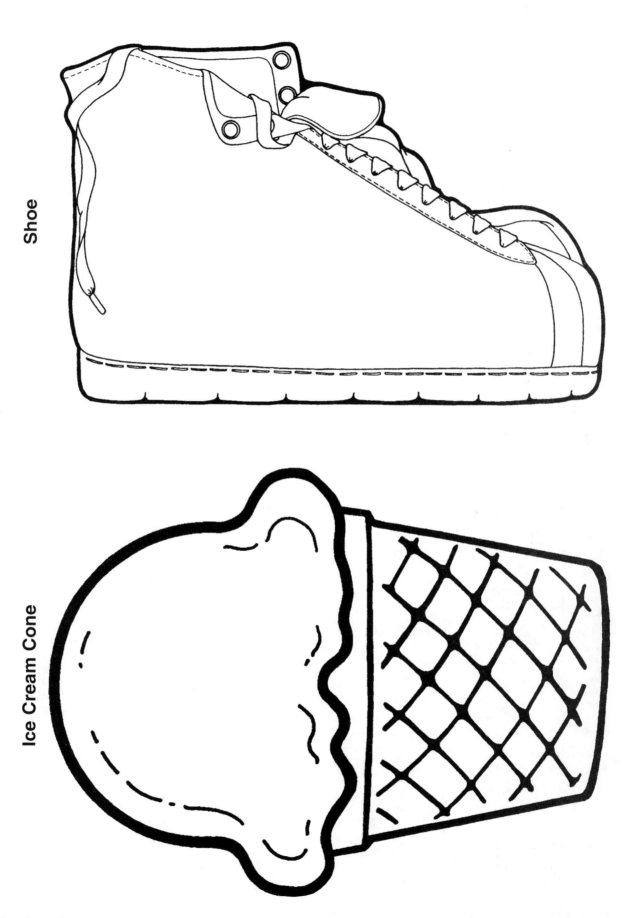

Pocket Chart Sentence Strips

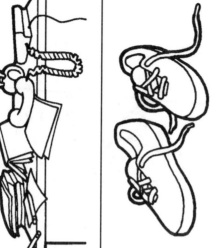
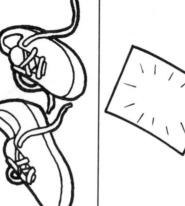

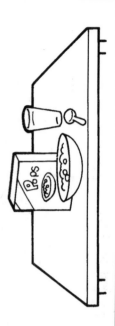

Alexander messed up his dad's office.

Alexander had to get plain white sneakers.

Alexander drew an invisible castle.

Alexander's mom said there are bad days in Australia, too.

Alexander didn't get a prize in his cereal.

Pocket Chart Sentence Strips *(cont.)*

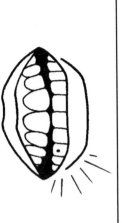

The dentist found a cavity in Alexander's tooth.

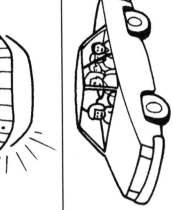

Alexander got carsick on the way to school.

Alexander had lima beans for dinner.

Alexander had no dessert in his lunch.

Alexander woke up with gum in his hair.

Story Questions

I. Knowledge (ability to recall information)

- What happened to Alexander when he first got up?
- Something happened to Alexander at each meal. Name the things that happened at breakfast, lunch, or dinner.
- Name two things that happened to Alexander at school.
- To what three places did Alexander's mom take him and his brothers after school?
- Where did Alexander keep saying he was going to go?

II. Comprehension (basic understanding of information)

- Besides "bad" or "terrible," how could you describe how Alexander was feeling?
- Why does Alexander keep saying he's going to Australia? Do you think he means it? Why or why not?
- Why do you think no one listened when Alexander kept saying he was having a bad day?
- Do you think Alexander's friends and family understood how he was feeling? Why or why not?

III. Application (ability to do something new with information)

- What do you do when you are feeling sad or angry?
- Who helps you feel better when you're feeling angry or sad?
- Name something you have done to help someone else feel better.
- Where could Alexander really go (besides Australia) to get away from his problems and feel better?
- Where is a special place that you go to feel better if you're feeling bad?

IV. Analysis (ability to examine the parts of a whole)

- Which of Alexander's problems do you think was his biggest or worst? Why?
- Which of Alexander's problems do you think was his smallest? Why?
- Do you think any of the things that happened to Alexander were his fault? If yes, which ones and why?

V. Synthesis (ability to bring together information to make something new)

- How do you think Alexander's day might have been different if he had found a prize in his cereal or Paul had played with him at recess?
- What might have happened differently to make his day better?
- What could Alexander do to make the next day better?
- If you were Alexander's friend, what would you do to help him feel better?

VI. Evaluation (ability to form and defend an opinion)

- Do you think Alexander's family members were fair to him? Why or why not?
- Do you think Alexander's day was really as bad as he thought it was? Why or why not?

Stick Puppet Theaters

Make a class set of puppet theaters (one for each child) or make one theater for every 2–4 children.

Materials

22" x 28" (56 cm x 71 cm) pieces of colored poster board (enough for each student or group of students); markers, crayons, or paints; scissors or craft knife

Directions

1. Fold the poster board about 8" (20 cm) in from each of the shorter sides.

2. Cut a "window" in the center of the theater, large enough to accommodate two or three puppets. (See illustration.)

3. Let the children personalize and decorate their own theaters.

4. Laminate the theaters to make them more durable. You may wish to send the theaters home at the end of the year or save them to use year after year.

Suggestions for Using the Puppets and Puppet Theaters

Prepare the stick puppets, using the directions on page 22. Use the puppets and the puppet theaters with the readers' theater script on pages 43–45. (Let small groups of students take turns reading the parts and using the stick puppets.)

Let children experiment with the puppets by telling the story in their own words.

Read quotations from the book or make statements about the characters and ask students to hold up the stick puppets represented by the quotes or statements.

Stick Puppet Patterns

Directions: Reproduce the patterns on cardstock or construction paper. Color the patterns. Cut along the dotted lines. To complete the stick puppets, glue each pattern to a tongue depressor, craft stick, Popsicle stick, or plastic straw. Use the stick puppets with stick puppet theaters (page 21) and/or the readers' theater script (pages 43–45).

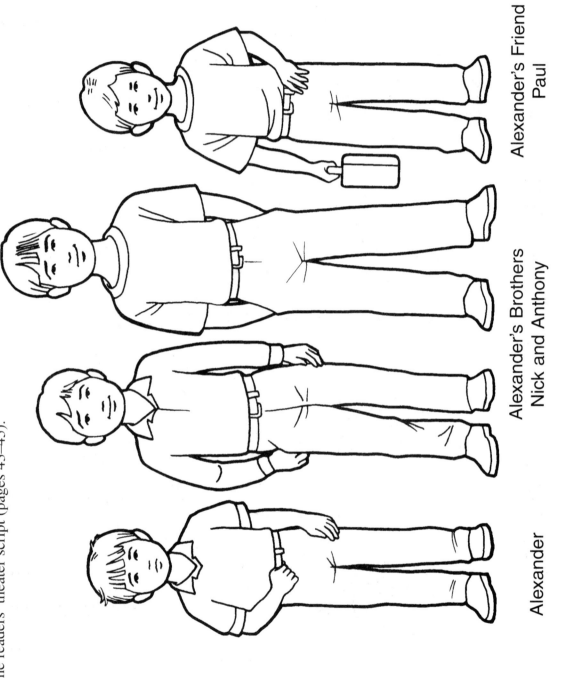

Alexander's Friend
Paul

Alexander's Brothers
Nick and Anthony

Alexander

Stick Puppet Patterns *(cont.)*

See page 22 for directions.

Mom   Dad   Teacher   Dentist

Journal and Creative Writing Ideas

Here are some ideas you may wish to use in your journals or for other creative writing activities. You may be asked to write on your own, to work in pairs or small groups, or to complete a writing activity as a whole class.

- Write about the worst day you ever had. Have any of the things that happened to Alexander ever happened to you?

- Write about the best day you ever had. What things happened? Where were you? Who else was there?

- Alexander hated the lima beans his family had for dinner. What is your favorite dinner? Write a menu for a great dinner for Alexander, listing all your favorite foods. Don't forget to illustrate your menu.

- Alexander wanted to go to Australia to get away from his problems. Where do you go to get away from your problems? Write about a place that is special for you. Where would you like to go if you could go anywhere in the world? Why would you like to go there?

- Alexander didn't want to move away from his friends and his neighborhood in the book *Alexander, Who's Not (Do you hear me? I mean it!) Going to Move*. Tell about the people and places you would miss most if you had to move, or tell about a time when you already moved.

- Pretend Alexander meets Ronald Morgan from the book *Today Was a Terrible Day*. Do you think they would be friends? What would they say to each other? What would they do together?

- Pretend you are Alexander. Write a letter to your friend Paul, telling him how you feel about his not wanting to be your best friend anymore. What could you say to convince him to be your best friend again?

- In all of Judith Viorst's Alexander books, Alexander has some problems with his brothers. What advice can you give Alexander to help him get his brothers to stop teasing him?

- Poor Alexander had a really bad day. Can you make tomorrow a better day for him? Write a story about Alexander's wonderful day. You can use the story map to help you get started.

Story Map

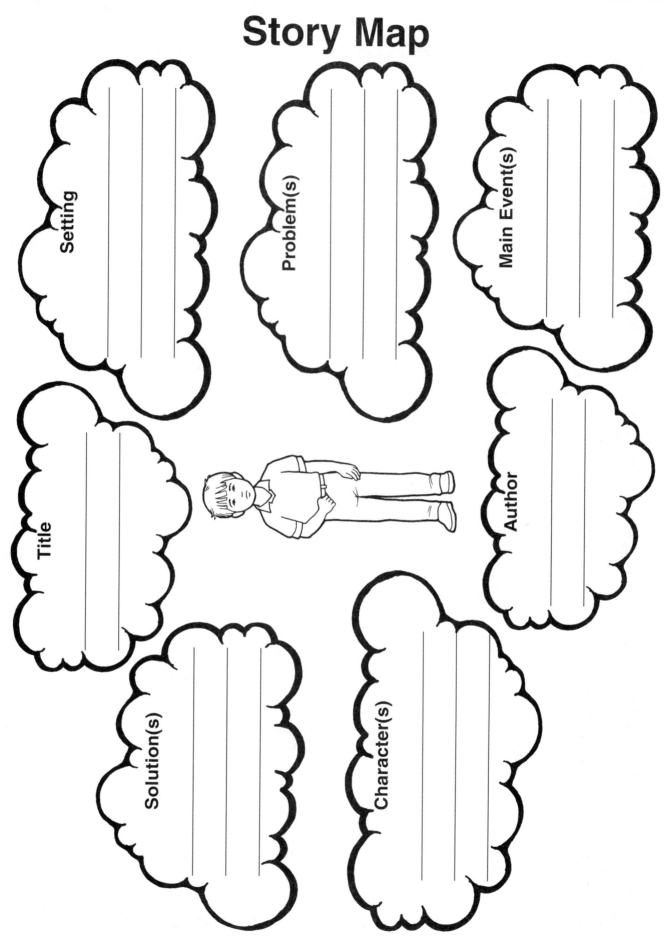

Setting

Problem(s)

Main Event(s)

Title

Author

Solution(s)

Character(s)

The Alexander Rap

1

Alexander was a good kid
Who had a bad day.
It didn't seem like anything
Was going his way.
"I'm going to Australia,"
He started to say.

2

He woke up with his chewing gum
Stuck in his hair.
He tripped over his skateboard,
Not knowing it was there.
He said, "I'm going to Australia,
This really isn't fair."

3

The day got even worse
On his way to school.
He felt like he was getting sick
While in the carpool.
He said, "I'm moving to Australia.
I know there it will be cool."

4

Things didn't get much better
At school that awful day.
No dessert in his lunchbox,
His best friend wouldn't play.
"I'm going to Australia,"
His teacher heard him say.

5

After school his day continued
To be extremely grim.
The dentist found a cavity
Only in him.
He said, "I'm going to Australia,
Even if I have to swim."

6

His brand new shoes were plain old
white,
Not blue or red or gray.
He said, "You can't make me wear
them,
Uh-uh, no way!"
"I'm running to Australia,"
The shoe man heard him say.

7

A disaster at Dad's office,
Lima beans on his plate,
Kissing on TV,
His day had not been great.
He said, "I'm going to Australia,
I really can't wait!"

8

He had a terrible, horrible,
No good, bad day.
"I'm going to Australia,"
His mom heard him say.
She said, "Even in Australia
There are days like today."

—*Diane Porteous*

Get the Scoop!

Help Alexander have a better day by making him an eight-decker ice-cream cone. First, color the scoops to make some delicious ice-cream flavors. Then, cut and paste the scoops onto the cone to show the events of the story in order from top to bottom. Don't let the ice cream fall off the cone!

Homophone Pairs

Choose the correct homophone for each word and write it on the matching shoe.

sundae   sail   too   buy   there   no   week   one

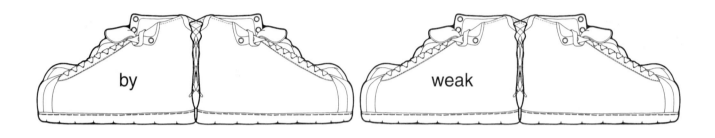

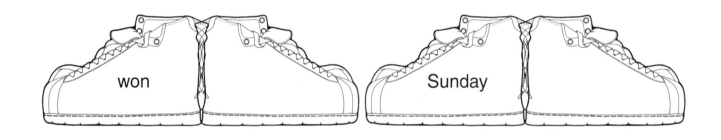

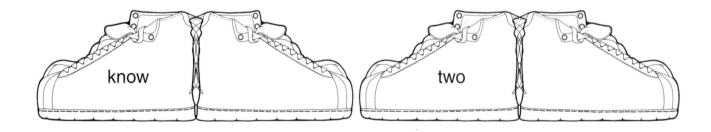

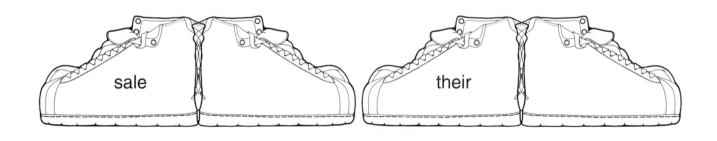

Time for Lunch!

In the book *Alexander, Who Used to Be Rich Last Sunday*, Alexander did not make good choices when spending his dollar.

Help him spend his money wisely by choosing good foods for his lunch. Choose one item from each row on page 30. Cut and paste them in the boxes below. Then, from page 31, cut and paste the correct coins to pay the exact amount for Alexander's lunch. Remember, you can spend no more than $1.00.

Entree	Vegetable

Fruit	Drink

Dessert

Total Cost $_____._____

Paste your coins here or on the back.

Time for Lunch! *(cont.)*

Entrees			
 taco (25 cents)	 hot dog (20 cents)	 pizza (25 cents)	 hamburger (20 cents)

Vegetables			
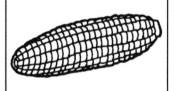 corn (10 cents)	 beans (15 cents)	 salad (15 cents)	 carrots (10 cents)

Fruits			
 banana (7 cents)	 apple (12 cents)	 peaches (8 cents)	orange (11 cents)

Drinks			
white milk (20 cents)	chocolate milk (20 cents)	orange juice (15 cents)	apple juice (15 cents)

Desserts			
 chocolate cake (25 cents)	 ice cream (20 cents)	 apple pie (25 cents)	 cookie (15 cents)

Time for Lunch! *(cont.)*

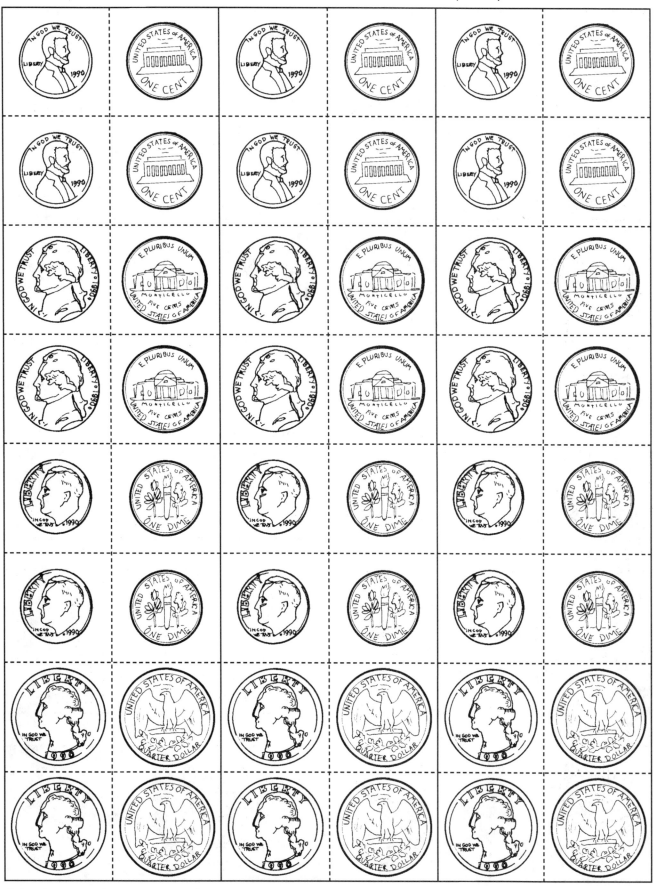

A Sundae on Sunday

In the book *Alexander, Who Used to Be Rich Last Sunday*, Alexander had exactly $1.00 to spend. Pretend you are Alexander and you would like to buy an ice-cream sundae. You can spend no more than $1.00. Check the prices for sundae ingredients on the ice-cream parlor chart below. Fill in the blanks on page 33 and then from page 31 cut out the correct coins for the exact amount of your sundae. Paste them on the bottom of page 33. Then make your sundae and enjoy it!

_____'s Ice-Cream Parlor

Ice Cream . . . . 25 cents a scoop (limit 2 scoops)

Chocolate Syrup . . . . 12 cents a squirt (limit 2 squirts)

Strawberry Syrup . . . . 9 cents a squirt (limit 2 squirts)

Sprinkles . . . . 7 cents a spoonful (limit 2 spoonfuls)

Whipped Topping . . . . . 6 cents a spoonful (limit 2 spoonfuls)

Bananas. . . . . 2 cents a slice (limit 6 slices)

A Sundae on Sunday (cont.)

_____'s Ice Cream Sundae

I will buy_____scoops of ice cream for_____cents per scoop.

I will spend this much for ice cream. ☐cents

I will buy_____squirts of chocolate syrup for_____cents per squirt.

I will spend this much for chocolate syrup. ☐cents

I will buy_____squirts of strawberry syrup for_____cents per squirt.

I will spend this much for strawberry syrup. ☐cents

I will buy_____spoonfuls of sprinkles for_____cents.

I will spend this much for sprinkles. ☐cents

I will buy_____spoonfuls of whipped topping for_____ cents.

I will spend this much for whipped topping. ☐cents

I will buy_____slices of banana for_____cents per slice.

I will spend this much for bananas. _____cents

I will spend this total amount for my sundae. $_____

Cut and paste your coins here. Make sure they match the exact total amount for the cost of your sundae.

Tin Can Ice Cream

Ingredients

- 1 cup (250 mL) milk
- 1 cup (250 mL) whipping cream
- ½ (125 mL) cup sugar
- ½ (2.5 mL) teaspoon vanilla

You will also need crushed ice, rock salt (table salt may be substituted), a one-pound and a three-pound coffee can for every four to five children.

Procedure

Put all ingredients in a one-pound coffee can with a tight-fitting plastic lid. Place the lid on the can and seal it tightly with masking tape. Place the can inside a three-pound coffee can with a tight-fitting plastic lid. Pack crushed ice around the outside of the small can. Pour at least ¾ cup of rock salt evenly over the ice. Place the lid on the outside can. Roll it back and forth on a table or the floor for 10 minutes. Open the outer can and carefully remove the inner can. Remove the tape, being very careful not to allow any salt water to get into the ice-cream mix. Use a rubber spatula to stir the mixture and scrape the sides of the can. Replace the lid and reseal it with tape. Drain the ice water from the large can. Replace the small can into the large can and repack it with ice and salt. Roll the can back and forth for another 10 minutes. Remove the inner can carefully. You should have a creamy, soft-serve type ice cream. Makes about three cups.

A Neighborhood Grid Map

	1	2	3	4	5	6	7
E		Seymour ⬛ Cleaners	Shoestore 👟				
D						Soccer ⚽ Field	
C			Dentist 🦷 Office				
B						🏫 School	
A	Alexander's House						

1. Draw Alexander's house in square A1. Draw his friend Paul's house next door in square A2.

2. In which square is the dentist's office? _____

3. Which business is located in square E3?_____

4. In which square is Seymour Cleaners? _____

5. In what two squares is the school located? _____

6. Draw playground equipment in the squares behind the school. What squares are these?_____

7. Draw Pearson's Drugstore in square D2.

8. Draw Friendly Market next door to the shoe store. In which square did you draw it?_____

9. If Alexander walks out his back door, which squares would he go through to school?_____

10. Draw an ice-cream store somewhere on the map. In which square did you draw it? _____

Answers: Fold under before reproducing.

2. C3   3. Shoestore   4. E2   5. B6, B7   6. C6, C7   8. E4   9. B1–B6

About Australia

Australia, the land "down under," is a country, an island, and a continent. It is about the size of the continental United States and is located in the southern hemisphere "down under" the equator and many of the world's other lands.

In 1770 Captain James Cook explored the eastern shores of the continent and claimed this land for Great Britain, calling it "New South Wales." The earliest British settlements were colonies for convicts, but free settlers soon began to make their homes there, setting up farms and searching for minerals. By 1827 Great Britain had claimed the entire continent and named it *Australia* from the Latin word *australis*, meaning "southern." Gold was discovered in the 1850s. Australia became independent on January 1, 1901.

Australia's citizens now include not only British immigrants, but many from Europe and Asia as well. The *Aborigines*, coming from Asia, were the original settlers of Australia. They lived in the open country where they hunted and fished to survive. Many were killed when British settlers came. The Aborigines were the inventors of the *boomerang*, a clublike weapon which returns to the person who throws it, and the *didgeridoo*, a long tube-shaped instrument made from a hollowed-out stick. The Aborigines now live throughout Australia, some on special reserves. Some Aborigine children are taught in schools on these reserves.

About Australia *(cont.)*

Australia has six states—Western Australia, South Australia, Queensland, New South Wales, Victoria, and Tasmania, and two territories—the Northern Territory and the Capital Territory, a small area south of the nation's capital of Canberra. Most of Australia's people live in the cities and towns in the eastern coastal area near the Great Dividing Range. This is a mountain range stretching from the Cape York Peninsula in Queensland to the south coast of Tasmania. The largest cities located in this eastern region include the ports of Sydney in New South Wales, Brisbane in Queensland, and Melbourne in Victoria. The rest of the continent, with the exception of a few low mountains including Ayers Rock located in the Northern Territory, is flat and fairly dry. The Great Artesian Basin is an area of plains west of the Great Dividing Range, below which lie rocks containing a large water supply. The water sometimes flows to the surface naturally and sometimes must be pumped. It is too salty for people to drink or to irrigate farmland but can be drunk by livestock. One third of Australia in the center of the continent is a desert which the Australians call "the outback" because it is out in the back of the mountains and cities. There are some areas in the outback and the plains where enough grass grows to raise sheep and cattle. They are raised on ranches called *stations*. Australia raises more sheep than any other country in the world.

Australia is home to many wild animals unique to the continent, including various marsupials such as kangaroos, koalas, Tasmanian devils, wallabies, and wombats, as well as the second largest bird in the world, the emu. The only egg-laying mammals (monotremes), the platypus and the echidna, also live in Australia.

The Great Barrier Reef is a series of reefs and small islands located off the northeastern coast of Australia. It is 1,250 miles long, making it the longest reef in the world. The reefs are formed by the skeletons of dead corals which stack up on top of each other. They are brightly colored, as are the tropical fish which live among them. The clear-water coral reefs are a big tourist attraction. It is a popular area for visitors and native Australians to enjoy the many water sports which are a favorite pastime in the country.

Australia's seasons are the reverse of countries in the northern hemisphere. Winter, which is fairly mild, is in June, July, and August; and summer is in December, January, and February. Australia's land and wildlife make it unique in many ways, but Australia's modern cities are very similar to those in America and Europe. Sydney, the largest city, is world famous for the Sydney Opera House, a spectacular structure with soaring, sail-like roofs, perched on the edge of a beautiful harbor. Many of the world's great singers, musicians, and composers have performed or had their works performed here. Australia is a diverse, fascinating, and beautiful continent.

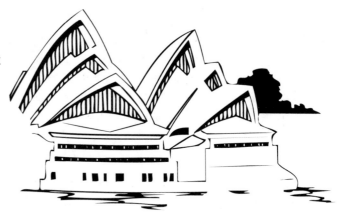

Australian Vocabulary

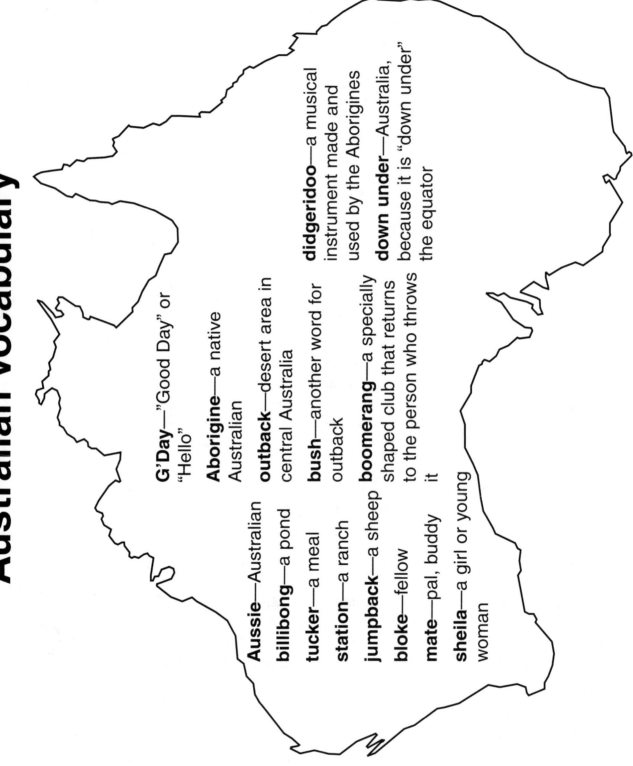

G'Day—"Good Day" or "Hello"

Aborigine—a native Australian

outback—desert area in central Australia

bush—another word for outback

boomerang—a specially shaped club that returns to the person who throws it

didgeridoo—a musical instrument made and used by the Aborigines

down under—Australia, because it is "down under" the equator

Aussie—Australian

billibong—a pond

tucker—a meal

station—a ranch

jumpback—a sheep

bloke—fellow

mate—pal, buddy

sheila—a girl or young woman

Name_____

Australia—Map Activity

Using the clues below, label Australia's states and territories.

1. Western Australia is the largest state.

2. Tasmania is the smallest state and an island.

3. Victoria is the small state just north of Tasmania.

4. Queensland is the large state near the Great Barrier Reef.

5. The Northern Territory lies between Western Australia and Queensland.

6. New South Wales is on the eastern coast and is where the Australian capital of Canberra is located.

7. The Capital Territory is a small area south of Canberra.

8. The state of South Australia borders the Northern Territory and all the other states except Tasmania.

Bonus Questions

9. Find a map of Australia in your classroom or at the library. Locate the Great Dividing Range. Add this mountain range to your map.

10. What oceans surround Australia? Add their names to your map.

11. Find the name of the large rock located in central Australia and label it on your map.

How Far Is 1,000 Miles Away?

(See directions in #4, page 12.)

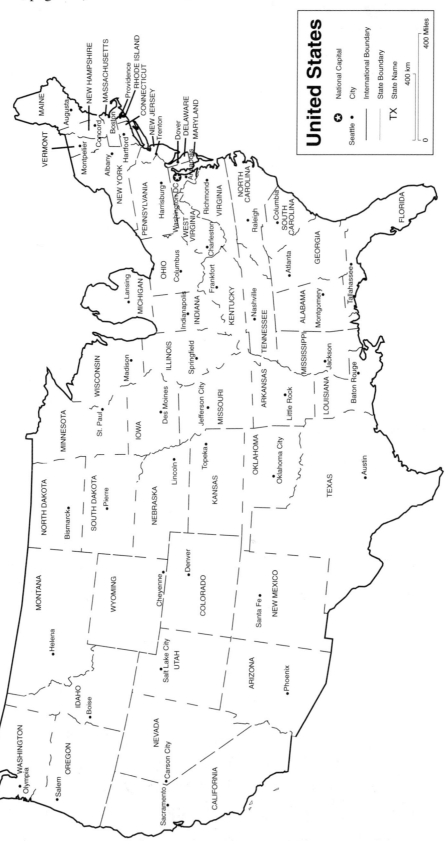

Aussie Animals

Cut out the pictures of these Australian animals and follow the directions on page 42.

Platypus

Frilled Lizard

Sheep

Koala

Tasmanian Devil

Wombat

Dingo

Emu

Kangaroo

Echidna

Aussie Animals *(cont.)*

Cut out the paragraphs below, match them to the correct animals on page 41, and paste them together on a large sheet of paper.

I am a mammal. I live on ranches called stations. More animals like me are raised in Australia than in any other country. I am raised for my wool and my meat.	I am a mammal and a marsupial. I eat leaves from eucalyptus trees. I often carry my baby on my back. I am not a bear, even though I may look like one.
I am a mammal and a marsupial. I look fierce, but I am not really a hunter. I eat remains of dead animals. I live on a small island called Tasmania.	I am an egg-laying mammal. I live on land, but I swim in the water. I have a beak and feet like a duck and a tail like a beaver.
I am an egg-laying mammal. I have a long tube-shaped snout that helps me find delicious ants. I have spines like a porcupine.	I am a reptile. I live in the outback. I can grow to be three feet long. I have a big collar around my neck called a frill. I stick it out to scare my enemies.
I am a mammal. I live in the outback. I prey on other mammals. I am a wild dog brought to Australia by the Aborigines.	I am the largest bird in Australia and the second largest in the world. I can weigh up to 120 pounds. I can run 30 miles an hour, but I can't fly.
I am a mammal and a marsupial. My baby is called a "joey." My long back legs help me hop as far as 30 feet in one bounce. I come in many colors, including gray and red.	I am a mammal and a marsupial. I look like a woodchuck. I burrow in the ground. My teeth are always growing, but they wear down when I eat.

Readers' Theater

Readers' Theater is an easy and enjoyable way for students to gain experience performing in front of a small audience. It is not necessary to have students memorize the dialogue or to use costumes or props. See page 13 for suggestions.

Alexander Goes Down Under
Characters

Alexander	Alexander's Classmates:
Alexander's Mom	Paul
Alexander's Dad	Albert
Alexander's Brothers:	Phillip
Nicholas	Olivia
Anthony	Sophie
Alexander's Teacher—Ms. Strictly	Elizabeth
Narrator	

Scene I—At Home

Narrator: G'Day mates! Welcome to our play. We hope you will enjoy our performance of "Alexander Goes Down Under." Our play starts at Alexander's house. Alexander and his parents and his two brothers are having dinner. Alexander doesn't look very happy.

Dad: Well, boys, how was school today?

Nicholas: Great! I hit a home run at recess.

Anthony: My day was pretty good, too. I only missed one word on my spelling test. (Alexander just picks at his food and sulks.)

Mom: Alexander, please stop picking at your food and sit up and eat. Do you feel all right?

Alexander: I feel O.K.

Mom: Then what's wrong?

Alexander: Ms. Strictly put us into groups and told us we have to do a report on a foreign country.

Dad: Well, that sounds like it could be fun.

Alexander: Maybe for you. I think it sounds like a lot of work.

Mom: What country did your group choose?

Alexander: That's just it. We can't even agree on a country to do. Phillip wants to report on a country with a lot of animals. Paul thinks we should stick to a place where they speak English. The girls want to report on a country with nice beaches. I don't think we'll ever agree.

Reader's Theater *(cont.)*

Nicholas: Alexander, you guys are so dorky. You already have agreed.

Alexander: What do you mean?

Nicholas: It's simple. Do your report on Australia. It has all those things.

Anthony: Yeah, Alexander, you're always saying you're going to go there.

Alexander: But I don't know anything about Australia. I don't even know where it is. I just know it's far away.

Dad: All the more reason to do a report about it. You can learn all about Australia and decide if you really want to go there someday.

Alexander: Well, I guess that's a good idea, but where do I start?

Mom: I suggest that you call your friends first and see if they want to report on Australia. Then, why don't you call your Aunt Margie? She's a travel agent, you know. I bet she has some information that could help you.

Alexander: Great idea, Mom! I'll go call Paul right now. May I be excused?

Mom: After you finish your lima beans.

Anthony: And don't forget, it's your turn to clear the table.

Alexander: Australia is sounding better all the time . . . .

Scene II—At School

Narrator: It is now one week later. Alexander and his classmates are giving their group reports.

Ms. Strictly: Nice job, kids. That was a great report on Mexico. I think we have time for our last group's report before lunch. Alexander, is your group ready?

Alexander: Yes, Ms. Strictly. Our report is on Australia. I'll start.

Ms. Strictly: Great, Alexander. Go ahead.

Alexander: Australia is the only country that is also a whole continent. It is an island, too. It is called the land "down under" because it is down under the equator and just about every place else in the world. It is about the size of the United States without Alaska and Hawaii. It is surrounded by the Indian Ocean on the west and the Pacific Ocean on the north and east. These two oceans come together and kind of mix up south of Australia.

Olivia: Australia was first used by Great Britain as a place to send prisoners. It became an independent country in 1901. Australia has six states and two territories. Its capital is Canberra.

Readers' Theater *(cont.)*

Albert: The Aborigines were the first people to live in Australia. They came from Asia and settled in the outback, where some of them still live. They invented the boomerang and the didgeridoo. That's an instrument made from a long hollowed-out stick.

Paul: Most of Australia's people live in the cities and towns near the east coast. There is a long mountain range that runs all up and down the country near the east coast, too. It's called The Great Dividing Range because it divides the part of Australia where most people live and the "outback." The outback is a big area in the middle of Australia that has some grassy plains and a lot of desert.

Phillip: A lot of really neat animals live in Australia. Most of them live in the outback. They have a lot of marsupials there. Marsupials are animals that carry their babies in a pouch. Some of them are kangaroos, wombats, koalas, and Tasmanian devils. The only two egg-laying mammals in the world live in Australia, too. They are the platypus and the echidna.

Elizabeth: In Australia the seasons are the opposite of ours. Their winter is in June, July, and August, and their summer is in December, January, and February. Australia has more sheep than any other country in the world. People raise them on ranches called stations.

Sophie: Australia has the biggest and prettiest coral reef in the world. It is called The Great Coral Reef. It's 1,250 miles long. It's made from lots of skeletons of dead corals piled up on top of each other. The corals are very colorful. Lots of colorful fish live there, too. People like to go there to swim and snorkel and scuba dive.

Alexander: My Aunt Margie is a travel agent. She told me it takes about 14 hours to fly to Sydney, Australia, from Los Angeles, California. That's about a 7,500 mile flight. It costs over $1,000 to fly there.

Ms. Strictly: Great report, Alexander. You and your friends have done an excellent job. You've made me want to take a trip to Australia someday.

Alexander: Me, too! But I guess I'll have to find a way to earn some money. I don't think my bus tokens will get me very far, unless Aunt Margie can get me a special deal!

Narrator: I hope you have enjoyed our play. We would now like to sing you a song about the story *Alexander and the Terrible, Horrible, No Good, Very Bad Day*. It's called, "Alexander Was Having a Bad Day."

Alexander Was Having a Bad Day

(to the tune of "My Bonnie Lies Over the Ocean")

Alexander was having a bad day,
Nothing was going quite right.
It started first thing in the morning,
And went on until late at night.

— Chorus —
Alexander was having a very bad day, bad day.
He kept saying he wanted to move far away.

His school day was not much fun either,
When counting he got quite confused.
He drew an invisible castle.
His teacher just wasn't amused.

(Chorus)

He had to go visit the dentist,
Who found a bad tooth in his mouth.
"Come back and I'll fix it next Thursday."
"By then I will be moving south."

(Chorus)

On the way home they stopped at the shoe store.
He had to buy shoes that were white,
Then on to his dad's busy office,
The mess Alex made was a sight.

(Chorus)

At home things did not get much better,
Gross lima beans upon his plate,
Disgusting TV shows with kissing,
"When will this day end? I can't wait!"

(Chorus)

He said he would move to Australia
And leave all his problems behind.
His mom told him that in Australia,
They had many days of this kind.

(Chorus)

—Diane Porteous

Alexander Center Activities

Draw a *visible* castle that Alexander's teacher might like better than his *invisible* one.

Design for Alexander a pair of really cool gym shoes that are *not* plain white.

In *Alexander Who Used to Be Rich Last Sunday*, Alexander did not spend his money wisely. List and illustrate at least five things that Alexander could buy with his $1.00 that would be better choices than the ones he made.

In *Alexander, Who's Not (Do you hear me? I mean it!) Going to Move*, Alexander didn't want to leave his old house and his friends. Draw a floor plan for Alexander's new bedroom in his new house that he'll like even better than his old room.

Bibliography

Other Books by Judith Viorst

Alexander, Who Used to Be Rich Last Sunday. Atheneum, 1978.

Alexander, Who's Not (Do you hear me? I mean it!) Going to Move. Atheneum, 1995.

Earrings. Atheneum, 1990.

The Good-bye Book. Atheneum, 1988.

If I Were in Charge of the World and Other Worries. Poems for Children and Their Parents. Atheneum, 1981.

I'll Fix Anthony. Harper, 1969. Macmillan, 1988.

My Mama Says There Aren't Any Zombies, Ghosts, Vampires, Creatures, Demons, Monsters, Fiends, Goblins or Things. Macmillan, 1988.

Sad Underwear: More Poems for Children and Their Parents. Atheneum, 1995.

Sunday Morning. Harper, 1968.

The Tenth Good Thing About Barney. Macmillan, 1988.

Try It Again, Sam: Safety When You Walk. Lothrop, 1970.

Rosie and Michael. Atheneum, 1974.

Related Literature

Giff, Patricia Reilly. *Today Was a Terrible Day.* Viking Press, 1982.

Schwartz, David. *If You Made a Million.* Scholastic, 1989.

Sharmat, Marjorie Weinman. *Mitchell Is Moving.* Macmillan, 1978.

Video Tapes

Alexander and the Terrible, Horrible, No Good, Very Bad Day. Based on the book by Judith Viorst. Home Box Office (HBO), 1990. 30 minutes.

Wonders Down Under, Really Wild Animal Series. National Geographic, 1993. 45 minutes.

Cassette Tapes

Around the World and Back Again. Tom Chapin. Sony, 1996. Excellent children's recording. Includes the song "What Is a Didjeridoo?"

Didgeridoos—Sounds of the Aborigine. Murdo McRae. Nesak International.

Music of My People—Australian Aboriginal Music. Bob Maza, Twintrack Productions.

Voices of the Dreamtime. Ross Lew Allen. Lotus, 1989.

Wee Sing and Color Australia. Pamela Beall and Susan Nipp. Price Stern Sloan, Inc., 1988. Coloring includes words to all songs on the accompanying tape.

Instrumental rap music is available on cassette tape from:
Plank Road Publishing, Inc.
12237 Watertown Plank Road
P.O. Box 26627
Wauwatosa, WI 53226

Book Lures, Inc.
P.O. Box 0455
O'Fallon, MO 63366-1455
"Poetry Rock and Rap" and piano accompaniment to children's tunes.

Books About Australia

Nonfiction

Amazing Animals of Australia. National Geographic, 1984.

Ellis, Rennie. *We Live in Australia.* The Bookwright Press, 1983.

Georges, D.V. *A New True Book— Australia.* Children's Press, 1986.

James, Ian. *Inside Australia.* Franklin Watts, 1989.

Kelly, Andrew. *Countries of the World—Australia.* The Bookwright Press, 1989.

Reynolds, Jan. *Down Under: Vanishing Cultures.* Harcourt Brace Jovanovich, 1992.

Fiction

Fox, Mem. *Koala Lou.* Harcourt Brace Jovanovich, 1988.

Katz, Avner. *A Little Pickpocket.* Simon & Schuster, 1996.

Nunes, Susan. *Tiddalick the Frog.* Atheneum, 1989.

Roth, Susan L. *The Biggest Frog in Australia.* Simon & Schuster, 1996.

Vaughan, Marcia K. *Wombat Stew.* Silver Burdett, 1986.

Vyner, Sue. *Swim for Cover! Adventure on the Coral Reef.* Crown Pub., 1995.

Technology

The Earth, the Oceans, and Plants & Animals: interactive, curriculum oriented CD-ROMs. CLEARVIEW. Available from Educational Resources, (800)624-2926. CD-ROM

Explore—Australia. Learningways, Inc. Available from William K. Bradford Publishing Co., (800)421-2009. disk

From Alice to Ocean: Alone Across the Outback. Claris Corporation. Available from Educational Resources, (800)624-2926. CD-ROM

Impressions, My First World Atlas. Available from Educational Resources, (800)624-2926.

MacGlobe & PC Globe. Broderbund. Available from Learning Services, (800)877-9378. disk

Odell Down Under. MECC. Available from MECC, (800)685-MECC. disk

Where in the World Is Carmen Sandiego? Broderbund. Available from Troll, (800)526-5289. CD-ROM and disk

The following titles are available from Media Max, 1-800-347-4242:

The U.S. Geographical Map Program. disk

The U.S. States Map Program. disk

Australia. disk

Picture Atlas of the World—National Geographic. Mac/Win CD-ROM

Money Town. Davidson/Simon & Schuster. Win CD-ROM

The Magic School Bus Explores the Ocean. Mac/Win CD-ROM

My First Amazing World Explorer. Mac/Win CD-ROM